The Little
Book of
Meditation

If your mind is unsteady,
try to think with your heart.

The Little Book of Meditation

10 Minutes a Day to More Relaxation,
Energy and Creativity

Dr Patrizia Collard

An Hachette UK Company
www.hachette.co.uk

First published in Great Britain in 2019 by Gaia Books,
an imprint of Octopus Publishing Group Ltd

Carmelite House
50 Victoria Embankment
London EC4Y 0DZ
www.octopusbooks.co.uk

Distributed in the US by Hachette Book Group,
1290 Avenue of the Americas, 4th and 5th Floors, New York, NY 10104
Distributed in Canada by Canadian Manda Group
664 Annette Street, Toronto, Ontario, Canada M6S 2C8

ISBN 978-1-85675-398-2

A CIP catalogue record for this book is available from the British Library.

Printed and bound in China.

10 8 6 4 2 1 3 5 7 9

Publishing Director Stephanie Jackson
Art Director Juliette Norsworthy
Senior Editor Alex Stetter
Editor, German edition Dr Diane Zilliges
Translation from German Jackie Smith, in association with
First Edition Translations Ltd, Cambridge, UK
Illustrator Jenny Römisch, www.jenny-roemisch.de
Design and layout Guter Punkt, Munich, adapted by Rosamund Saunders
Production Controller Katie Jarvis

Contents

Introduction: What exactly is meditation?

Meditation is medicine for the mind and body. Practising meditation can help calm an agitated mind, an all too common feature of life in the 21st century. Our minds are working overtime as we tackle our to-do lists, deal with the multimedia onslaught of information and spend stressful days at work. It can often be difficult to find stillness, even for a moment, and to stop our thoughts from constantly spinning. But with a little practice we can learn to let go of our thoughts, allowing us to relax completely.

This little book gives you an introduction to various forms of meditation originating from different spiritual traditions, as well as some developed specially by stress-management experts. But what they all have in common is that they will help you be actively aware of each moment, and be present in the here and now. For this moment is when you truly experience your life, as you learn consciously to hear, to taste, to feel and actually to be, enabling you to shift out of autopilot for a while. Give it a try, and treat yourself to a few minutes of inner calm every day.

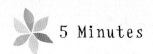 5 Minutes

First Exercise: A place where I can be relaxed and content

Sit yourself down comfortably in a quiet place and wrap yourself in a blanket. Softly close your eyes and relax your facial muscles. Let go of the tension in your neck, your shoulders and anywhere else that feels tense.

Now become aware of your breathing. Start taking slow, deep breaths in and out. With every inhale you receive fresh oxygen and a boost of energy. With every exhale you feel lighter and more at ease. Now imagine a place where you feel free and contented. Here are a few suggestions, but you are welcome to pick somewhere completely different:

- a cosy room with a wood fire glowing in the fireplace

- a sandy beach with palm trees and an azure blue sea

- a garden full of wonderful plants and flowers

- a quiet, peaceful forest with ferns, moss and animals

Imagine lingering in this place for a while. You are perfectly content and feel safe and calm. Start by taking note of all the images and things that catch your eye here. Become aware of them. Look at the colours; perhaps your favourite colour is among them.

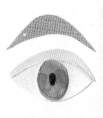

Now listen intently and notice the sounds around you. What can you hear? Maybe the wind, birdsong or the calls of animals, the sound of your own footsteps?

Breathe in again deeply through your nose, and take in the scents of this place. Enjoy all the different aromas. Is there a fragrance among them that you find particularly enticing or enchanting?

Does the air taste of salt, if you are near the ocean? What can you taste on your tongue? Did you perhaps pick a berry and take a bite?

Now touch something in your favourite place of relaxation. Pick up this object, feel its shape, its size, its weight and also what its surface feels like – rough, smooth, cold, warm, soft?

You have now anchored yourself to this place with all your senses. Take a few more deep breaths and be very aware of how everything feels at this moment. The more relaxed and contented you feel there, and the more often you repeat this exercise, the easier it will be for you to return to this relaxed state when you are in a difficult situation: you need only recall this magical place and your body will automatically relax. The more you practise, the sooner this reaction will become established. One month of daily practice and you will have created a new neural pathway – a direct route to a state of relaxation.

"If every eight-year-old in the world
is taught meditation, we will eliminate violence
from the world within one generation."

The effect of meditation

These days meditation is not only practised and appreciated
by more and more people, the world of science has also
recognized its potential and started researching it in depth.
Researchers working in the field of social neuroscience, such
as neurologist Professor Tania Singer, have been studying the
effects of meditation on the body, brain and the entire way
we experience life.

MRI (Magnetic Resonance Imaging) scans have revealed
marked changes in the brain structure of subjects who
regularly practise mindfulness meditation: the brain's density
increases in the areas responsible for creativity, short-term

memory, decision-making, empathy and self-compassion. Moreover, these people were observed to be generally less easily stressed, and less likely to produce adrenaline or cortisol. These two stress chemicals are helpful if you ever need to get away from a mugger, for example, but not when you need to think more clearly and creatively in order to identify opportunities, solve problems or master difficult challenges. A meditating mind is a creative and inventive mind, and helps us to be generally more understanding, affectionate, patient and empathetic.

Other benefits include improved immune responses and faster recovery from some medical conditions (for example, psoriasis, chronic pain and even some forms of cancer). Meditation can help lower your blood pressure and improve the quality of your sleep. There are also indications that meditation slows the ageing of the brain. What's more, people who practise meditation tend to form longer telomeres. According to the latest research, these particular DNA sections have the effect of helping us stay healthy for longer and of delaying the ageing process.

Neuroscientists have also demonstrated that meditation – and the use of mental images, in particular – has a therapeutic effect on the psyche. It has been shown that conscious visualizations generate very similar patterns of brain activity to events actually experienced. For example, by repeatedly visualizing a situation that makes us anxious (an exam, a job interview or something similar), we can condition the brain to be much less anxious about this situation. It is as if the brain has experienced it "enough times already", even if the event was only imagined.

Working in collaboration with Professor Herbert Benson, a neuroscientist at Harvard University, Tania Singer came to the conclusion that the brain accords visualizations similar status to actual memories of real events. If one visualizes emotions like peace, inner calm, being in harmony with oneself, fulfilment and love, sooner or later these same feelings will establish themselves in real life. It is important to emphasize, though, that you need to meditate quite regularly to achieve these results.

Although meditation is known to be a good thing, few people have a real understanding of how to make meditation a part of their lives, and what incredible opportunities it gives us to improve the way we live our lives. For instance, we can learn to block out unhelpful thoughts, to experience perfect tranquillity every now and then, to expand our awareness, or simply to relax our body and mind. The very first exercise, starting on page 7, will already have given you a sense of this.

How did meditation come to Europe?

In 1911, Hermann Hesse travelled to Ceylon (Sri Lanka). Drawing on this experience, in 1922 he completed his book *Siddhartha,* the life story of the historical figure Siddhartha Gautama, who later came to be known as the Buddha. This book is one of the most widely read works of the 20th century. Along with many others, Hesse awakened the growing interest of Westerners in Eastern wisdom and also in meditation.

Madonna does it; Hugh Jackman, Clint Eastwood, Nicole Kidman, Sting and Paul McCartney do it too. For me it was above all the Beatles, whose song lyrics I translated into my native German at the age of ten because I thought they were amazing. That was my first, indirect contact with meditation.

In the 1960s, a lot of people went on pilgrimages to India and studied yoga and Transcendental Meditation (TM) with Maharishi Mahesh Yogi. This guru had held a seminar in Bangor, North Wales, which the Beatles had attended. My idol, George Harrison, was at his most creative after he started practising meditation. He wrote 48 songs!

Many years later, in the mid-Eighties, Bangor University was where I took up my first academic position. Twenty years after that, Bangor became the centre for mindfulness meditation, the form of meditation that scientists have so far studied in greatest depth, and which today serves as a lifeline for many in times of crisis. It was in this wonderful place that I, too, trained as a teacher of meditation.

In the six chapters of this little book, I will be presenting a number of different meditations, designed to help you discover how you can make your "now" more peaceful, healthy and fulfilled. If you try the exercises and practise them repeatedly, your life can be more free of fear, stress, anger and boredom. You will better be able to focus on the things in life that really matter to you.

There are hundreds of ways of practising meditation. In this book, I have endeavoured to choose those you can easily incorporate into your daily life. A recently published study has shown that just ten minutes of meditation a day can bring about real changes.

What types of meditation are there?

There are many different forms of meditation, some active, some passive, including silent meditation, mindfulness meditation, dance meditation and other movement meditations, visualizations, mantras that can be spoken or chanted, and many, many others. We will be practising some of these forms of meditation together later.

Meditation covers a broad spectrum. In my own practice and in this book, I also use relaxation, affirmation and imagination techniques that are related to meditation in the strictest sense of the word. Meditations generally involve one or more of the senses, and may use images, language, sounds, taste sensations and smells.

How and when to meditate

Many of the exercises described here can be performed
virtually anytime, anywhere: when you are out and about,
waiting in a queue or stuck in traffic (provided you are not
the driver), when you fancy a quick break or when you are
feeling completely overwhelmed. But I have also chosen
some meditations that require a little more time and space.

Whether you like to meditate at the crack of dawn or late in the evening, or at some point in the afternoon to recharge your batteries, it is very useful to set up a special space for your meditation. It doesn't have to be a whole room, just a quiet place (perhaps a comfortable armchair) that your subconscious comes to regard as a place where you are safe and protected. By returning regularly to this place you will awaken habitual associations.

You may want to use a special shawl or a cosy blanket, and perhaps add a sea shell, a nice plant, a little indoor fountain, a candle or some other symbolic object that makes this particular spot a place of peace and tranquillity. You should feel completely comfortable – make sure, too, that you won't feel chilly. You could let others know, perhaps with a little sign on the door, that you do not want to be disturbed for a while. And switch off your phone before you start.

If possible, set aside a time slot every day for your meditation practice, at least for the first three weeks (and ideally for longer). Write it in your calendar. It is up to you to decide when to meditate and for how long. Give it a try and see what works best for you.

The same goes for the words I have suggested for certain meditations: choose your own words to ensure the exercises meet your particular needs. You know yourself best, after all.

I recommend keeping a meditation diary where you write down anything that strikes you as important. It can accompany you on this journey and will also help you remember the things you learn along the way. When we write things down, the thoughts lodge in our conscious mind, as this activity requires us to operate on several levels simultaneously: we are seeing, we are thinking, and we are physically touching the pen and paper. You may also like to use different colours, or add images or symbols that have meaning for you.

Treat yourself to a nice notebook, the mere existence of which will already be inspiring. Date your entries – this may turn out to be quite interesting later on, when you are perusing the book or flicking through the pages. Your journal will show you how meditation changes you, and encourage you to keep transforming your life. It can also be helpful to unburden yourself by writing down persistent negative thoughts. You can then leave them sitting on the pages of your diary until you decide to address them. Keeping this journal is a meditative exercise in itself.

Affirmations

An affirmation is a positive, consciousness-expanding thought that takes the place of negative thought patterns and judgments. You will find an affirmation at the beginning of each chapter. You can say your chosen words or phrases to yourself quietly or out loud, or just think them, but it is a good idea to write them down in your little practice book. I recommend five to ten repetitions, ideally at various points throughout the day, for example every time you wash your hands.

"I accept at this moment that the journey to myself will not always go smoothly. But I know how important it is for me to embark on it."

I wish you much pleasure and joy on this wonderful journey.

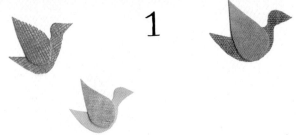

1

Reduce Stress and Strengthen Your Immune System

Too much work, a constant stream of new challenges, not enough sleep and hardly any time to relax? If this sounds familiar, you know that you can all too easily end up feeling overwhelmed and full of self-doubt, or even getting ill. This chapter contains exercises to help you handle these difficulties and strengthen your body's defences.

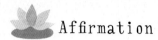 # Affirmation

"I create breathing spaces for myself every day.
Moments that I spend only in the here and now, when
I absorb all that is beautiful, kind and good in
this life and in turn offer it to others as well."

If you like, you can name things that bring you joy in this
affirmation – for example, the sun, the blue sky, the sea…

5 Minutes

Breathing space

Imagine an hourglass: the upper part contains everything you are experiencing, feeling or are aware of at this moment that is causing you distress. Hold all these things in your awareness for about one minute, or for about five to ten breaths. Take a look at them, whatever they are. Accept with all your senses these aspects of the present moment. This is simply the way things are right now.

Then picture the narrow neck of the hourglass, which symbolizes the point at which you let go of all thoughts as best you can and focus only on the breath. Breathe in and out slowly and calmly ten times and try to let any thoughts simply pass by.

Then, when you are hopefully already feeling more calm and serene, visualize the bottom third of the hourglass. This is the base and the centre of strength. As you look at it, become aware of your feet and let yourself feel grounded. Imagine you are growing roots that go deep into the ground and visualize a tree, the symbol of strength and fortitude. Or a mountain or a bear – whatever symbol works best for you.

It is very likely that at the end of this short exercise, you will be feeling stronger and more relaxed than before. And you were probably able to watch your anxious thoughts simply trickle from the top of the hourglass down to the bottom, where they can now stay.

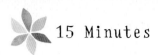 15 Minutes

Chakra meditation to strengthen body and mind

The word "chakra" comes from Sanskrit, the ancient Indian language that was used for holy and instructional writings in particular. "Chakra" means "wheel" or "vortex". According to yogic teaching, our body has seven of these energy points. The first is located at the base of the spine, at the tailbone, and the last on the top of the skull. Each chakra has its own colour: red, orange, yellow, green, blue, indigo and violet. When they are all in balance, we are healthy in both body and mind.

Find a comfortable seated position and close your eyes: feel your tailbone, where the *root chakra* is located. For the next five to ten breaths, imagine a kind of funnel projecting out backward from it, sucking in a spinning, whirling mass of red energy. It is a warming, healing energy. This chakra represents physical survival, vitality, patience, courage and material security. It strengthens our instincts and connects us strongly to the Earth. If you are lacking energy in this chakra, you may start experiencing foot, knee, pelvis and lower back problems.

When you feel you have absorbed enough root energy, mentally close this funnel and move up to the *sacral chakra*. This time picture a funnel opening up toward the front of your lower abdomen. This time the healing energy you absorb with every breath is orange. As before, keep breathing until you feel that the chakra is full. I recommend at least five to ten breaths. This chakra is associated with sexual power, creativity, new ideas, passion and endurance. When the sacral chakra is "empty", these qualities are barely available to us, and the organs of the lower abdomen (such as the kidneys, ovaries and prostate) may also be affected. Once again, mentally close this funnel once you feel a sense of comfort.

Now proceed in the same way with the third chakra, the *solar plexus chakra*. Located directly below the ribcage, it gives you a sense of your own identity. It fosters self-confidence, inner strength, humour, spontaneity and warmth of personality. When this chakra is out of balance, you may experience problems with your digestive system, liver or gall bladder. Again, imagine a funnel projecting out to the front, and as you inhale, absorb the spinning yellow energy until you feel a sense of comfort. Then close the funnel.

Next, visualize the *heart chakra*, which is further up, right in the centre of the chest. This is the centre of your self and your being. Through the heart chakra we feel sympathy and spread love and compassion. We can forgive others and ourselves. When it is out of balance, the heart and also the lungs may suffer.

Here, too, open a forward-facing funnel and breathe in green energy until you feel right again in this area.

Next comes the *throat chakra*. It helps us express our true selves and what we stand for. A healthy throat chakra helps us communicate with others and build bridges to our fellow human beings. When it is empty, you may experience problems with the throat, mouth or thyroid. Here you breathe in blue energy through the forward-facing funnel.

Next we work with the *third eye chakra*, which is located in the middle of your forehead, between your eyes. It is associated with intuition, self-knowledge and insight. When it is out of balance, the eyes, nose, ears and central nervous system may be impaired. Again, picture the funnel and breathe in the colour indigo until you feel good and fulfilled.

We finish with the *crown chakra*, which is located above the top of the head. It energizes many of our brain functions, fosters positive thinking and a spirit of inventiveness, as well as putting us in touch with our spirituality and humanity. When it is out of balance, you may suffer headaches and errors in reasoning. This time the funnel points upward toward the sky. Breathe in violet light until you feel perfectly balanced and calm. You never completely close this funnel, instead remaining permanently connected to the universe by a "silver beam".

Take your time with this meditation. It is one I recommend wholeheartedly. It balances your whole being and gives you a deep sense of peace.

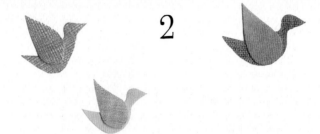

2

Gain Courage
and Self-confidence

We are constantly under pressure to prove how
much we can do and how independent we are.
Wouldn't everything be a lot easier if we could
understand that each of us is merely a part of the
whole? All we can offer the world are our own
individual talents.

Affirmation

"Today I will take a gentle
look at my 'wounds and scars'.
They will show me that even
a stony path brings adventure
and experiences. I notice the
things that are, have
been and will be
instructive and
wonderful."

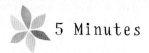

5 Minutes

Self-compassion break

Are you thinking about a difficult episode in your life that upsets or agitates you? Try not to suppress it, but to accept it. It is what it is: perhaps an argument with someone close to you, a loss, pain, whatever it may be.

Use the calming power of touch by giving yourself a hug. You can either place one hand on your heart and the other on your solar plexus, or you can place both hands on your cheeks and hold your face. Focus wholly on yourself as best you can.

Become aware that you are suffering or afraid in this moment. Say to yourself with your inner voice, "It hurts" or "Ouch" or something similar, as your way of expressing the thought that things are not well with you right now and that you are holding yourself to gain courage and strength.

Next, remember that everyone suffers sometimes, is afraid, feels inadequate or is in pain. Tell yourself, "I am not alone", or "I am not the only one to have problems. They are part of human life."

Finally, whisper affectionate, uplifting phrases or words to yourself: "May I feel safe and secure", "May I feel brave and strong", "May I feel peaceful and unburdened." Or just "inner peace", "safety", "relaxation", "contentment".

You are sure to feel more peaceful within just a few minutes.

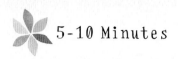

5-10 Minutes

Movement Meditation: Relax your neck and shoulders

When we are unhappy with ourselves and feel inadequate, our body produces certain chemicals – the same ones that are released when we feel fear or anger caused by an external trigger, for example, if an aggressive dog comes hurtling toward us. The body does not seem to be able to tell the difference between self-imposed negativity arising from self-criticism, feelings of shame and so on, and negative feelings resulting from external pressures.

When these chemicals (adrenaline and cortisol, in particular) are frequently released around our body, we become increasingly beset by gloomy thoughts and our body becomes more and more sluggish and tense. Whenever we put ourselves down, we need to reassure ourselves as soon as possible with love and compassion. A simple body meditation can work wonders.

Make sure you keep breathing normally throughout the exercise – in other words, don't hold your breath.

Part 1: Loosen up your neck and shoulders

Start standing up, with your feet hip width apart and parallel. As you inhale, slowly raise both arms in front of you up to chest height or even higher, so they are above your head, with your fingertips pointing toward the sky.

As you exhale, lower your arms back to their starting position, simply hanging down by your sides.

Repeat this sequence at least three times, and preferably more. If you cannot raise your arms all the way up, that is perfectly fine. Raise them as high as feels comfortable for you.

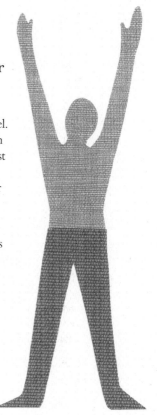

Let both arms dangle by the sides of your body, and perform a gentle neck exercise. The chin should be parallel to the ground, the facial muscles as relaxed as possible. Now breathe in slowly and, keeping them parallel to the ground, turn your chin and neck toward your right shoulder – only as far as you can go without discomfort. Bring them back to the centre as you breathe in, then on the next exhale turn toward the left.

Repeat these neck exercises three to five times in each direction. You may notice that your neck feels slightly more relaxed and you can move it a little further with each turn. This may or may not happen, as the case may be. Listen to your inner voice of wisdom.

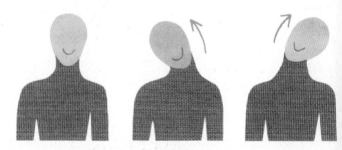

Part 2: Qigong massage

If possible, start with the right hand
and massage your left arm from
the shoulder down to the left
hand: you can massage and
lightly pat along the
inside and outside of your
left arm with a loose fist
or the flat of your hand.
Repeat this massage, going
down and up at least three
times. Then repeat with the left
hand on the right arm.

Now pat the tension out of
your upper body: start in the
area of the collarbones,
followed by the ribcage,
stomach and hips and maybe the
sides of your body, if you can reach
them easily, ideally going right down to the
lower back.

Now move on to your left leg,
patting and slapping it to relax the
front and the back. Go down as far
as possible. You can do this while
sitting down, if you prefer. Then
work on massaging the right leg.

Finally, using just
your fingertips,
massage and tap your
face and then the top
of your head, very gently.
It feels almost like lovely
warm raindrops pattering
down on you.

You can, of course, opt to massage only
those areas that you can reach with ease
and those where the resulting sense of
relief is most palpable.

Imagination:
I can do this

Do you have a presentation or
a job interview coming up, a meeting
or an exam that you don't want to mess
up? This exercise in imagination will help you
perform your best while maintaining your inner
calm. It can be used for any situation where you
want to make a good impression. However, you
have to practise it seven times in succession,
starting well in advance of the event in question.

This exercise in imagination is often used by
competitive athletes. For example, they might
visualize themselves running a 100-metre race
and crossing the finish line in exactly the time
they had been aiming for. They picture their
target time on a big clock!

In these instructions, I will use a presentation
you are preparing to give as an example. You
can substitute the details of your own particular
situation instead.

Sit up straight and close your eyes. Feel how
your body is connected to the surface you are
sitting on. Feel, too, how your feet are firmly
connected to the floor.

Now turn your eyes upward and inward without opening them, almost as though you were trying to look at your own brain. Even if it seems quite an effort, hold this position for three breaths, then, keeping your eyes closed, let them return to their starting position.

On the next exhalation, notice that you are feeling more and more relaxed. In your imagination, pat your forehead, your cheeks and your whole face, starting at the top and working your way down, and let yourself become even more relaxed with the next exhale. Your entire head and face now feel lighter, and with every exhale, you relax more and more deeply.

Now move on to the neck and spine. Imagine that you are starting to slowly pat and ease out these parts of the body: relax all 24 vertebrae, from the neck to the tailbone, let go and, with each exhalation, sink even more deeply into a state of relaxation.

Now mentally move on to the front of your upper body: soften and relax your shoulders, relax your ribcage, collarbones, abdominal wall, your hips and then your buttocks. Soften and relax all your muscles. Remember that you can go even deeper and let go even more with each exhale.

Now, working from the shoulders down, become aware of and relax your arms and hands. Finally, completely relax your thighs, lower legs, feet and toes. At the same time, keep your feet firmly grounded to support you.

Still keeping your eyes closed, imagine that you are sitting in a cinema with a huge blue screen. A film now starts playing on this screen: you see yourself, wearing the outfit you have picked for your big day. You can also see how you have styled your hair.

And now you open the door to the meeting room. There you see either a table, with your audience sitting around it, or a podium that you now walk confidently toward. You have written a few keywords on notecards, or maybe prepared some slides on your laptop. Everything is already plugged in. All you have to do is start.

Now you hear the beginning… and then the end of your presentation. Maybe also a few questions from people you may or may not know. You feel able to answer them calmly and clearly. It may also happen that you occasionally have to say, "I need to think about that", or "I'll get back to you about that in the next few days. I don't have the answer right now." That only makes you more human. No one can answer every question 100 percent every time. And even if there is a bit of a slip-up, that's fine. Take it with good humour and smile gently.

Finish this exercise by watching yourself leaving the room.

This internal film is a perfect way of preparing. The more often you watch it, the more your brain remembers that everything goes well.

 # 5 Minutes

Candle meditation

This simple but very effective meditation is particularly good for bringing us inner stillness and helping us be free of fear.

Sit at a table and light a candle. Consciously breathe in and out slightly more deeply than normal.

Focus on the candle flame and imagine its light flowing into you and becoming part of your being. You begin to feel the warmth inside you, and you start to relax more and more, from your head to your toes.

Now gently close your eyes and keep picturing the flickering light of the candle flame. Draw the light and the comforting warmth deeper and deeper into you, until you eventually feel as if you are actually one with the light. The healing, soothing light shines into you and out of you.

When you feel that everything inside you has settled down, that any troubling thoughts and unpleasant feelings have now been pushed to the back of your awareness, start to focus more on your breathing again, and notice your feet firmly anchored to the ground. Sit there for a while longer, following your breath, and then open your eyes.

Have a stretch, massage your face and finish by blowing out the candle.

3

Clear
Your Head

We cannot have peace of mind if our thoughts
keep racing. This is where meditation can help –
and the following exercises in particular.

Affirmation

"I promise myself that I will meditate regularly, regardless of my state of mind at the time. This promise in itself will help me let go of dark thoughts and feelings. I have an imaginary box where I can put unpleasant thoughts once I have had a good look at them. I find inner resources to help me keep making this box and its contents smaller."

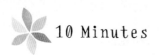

10 Minutes

Thoughts are not necessarily true

I invite you to go to your place of meditation, sit down and make yourself comfortable. Have a shawl or a blanket to hand if it is cool today, or as a prop to remind you why you are here.

Focus on the parts of your body that are in contact with the armchair or the floor: your back, your buttocks, and also your hands, which can either be folded in your lap, or resting on your thighs.

Try to relax your facial muscles and shoulders. Close your eyes, if that feels good to you, or leave them half-open without focusing on anything.

Become very aware of your breathing. You will notice that each breath is a unit in itself, longer or shorter, deeper or shallower. You will notice over time that after every inhale and exhale there is a brief pause before the "next round" begins. Follow your breathing until you feel a sense of calm.

Now turn your attention to your body. Do you feel any strong sensations anywhere? If you notice areas of tension or pain, you can try to breathe into these areas and, on each exhalation, let go of any tension as best you can.

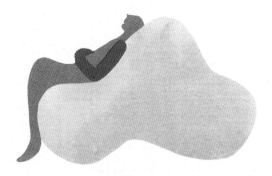

Now take a conscious look at your thoughts, especially any that trigger unpleasant feelings and bodily sensations. It is important to remember that your aim here is to recognize the thought patterns that oppress you and can sometimes drag you down into a black hole. If you manage to identify a pattern, you can make a note of it in your diary once you have finished meditating. What you are not aiming to do here is somehow magically change those thoughts. Your attitude is one of keen interest, while at the same time keeping a certain distance to ensure that you are not swept along by what might be a raging torrent.

There is a technique that meditation practitioners use to allow them to see their thoughts but not let them take control: they give them a name, which makes it possible to preserve the necessary distance. Thoughts can be negative, neutral or positive, of course. But whichever category they fall into, in this meditation you will only look at them briefly and give them a name.

Some people find the following images useful:

- You see the thoughts as clouds in the sky. You can see the labels for your thought patterns written in fluffy writing on these clouds: "brooding thoughts", "self-critical thoughts", "apocalyptic thoughts", "daydreams", "shopping lists" and so on.

- You are standing on a bridge and looking down at a small river with colourful leaves floating in it. You see your thoughts written on some of these leaves. You can read them and register them, but very soon the leaf has disappeared under the bridge.

- You are standing on a station platform. A train speeds past. You see the carriages and one of your thoughts is written on each one. You see what they allude to, but let your thoughts simply pass on by.

By repeatedly practising this meditation, you will learn that thoughts are not necessarily always true or important, and that you can decide which thoughts you want to turn your full attention to later, once you have finished meditating.

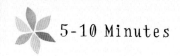 # 5-10 Minutes

Mountain visualization

Sit down on the floor with a blanket and one or two
cushions. Sit either cross-legged, or with your back against
the wall and your knees drawn up. Alternatively, you could
sit up straight on a chair.

Now visualize the most beautiful, awe-inspiring mountain
you know. Or try to imagine one, as best you can. The
mountain has a pointed or rounded summit, sloping sides
and a base.

Now try to project this image onto yourself: your head
becomes the summit, your shoulders and arms become
the sloping sides, and your buttocks and legs become the
base of this majestic formation.

Now picture the mountain on a mild spring day: there are
birds flying and small insects buzzing in the air, the trees and
shrubs all around and on the mountain slopes have begun to
sprout new leaves. Everything is flourishing. There is a smell
of lilac. A slight breeze is blowing.

The mountain stands majestically in the midst of this
wonderful tumult of activity. It remains motionless, as if
keeping watch over everything.

Now, in your mind's eye, change the season to a blazing hot summer's day. The sky is blue and the sun is at its zenith.

The air is heavy and oppressive. You see
butterflies in the air, bees searching for nectar,
and small animals scampering around on the
mountainside. All the colours of the rainbow are
gathered around you in the form of flowers and leaves.
The many different shades of green stand out especially:
deciduous and evergreen trees, grasses and ferns.

Again, the mountain looks imperturbable and majestic.
Again, it does not move, a sentry watching over the
natural world, as it has done for thousands
upon thousands of years.

Let this image fade into the background now, and next imagine a windy, rainy autumn day. The sky is covered with grey clouds, and the wind is blowing and whistling around the mountainside. All living creatures seem to have hidden themselves away. Colourful autumn leaves – green, yellow, red, brown and orange – swirl through the air. The branches of the trees and the taller bushes dance a wild autumn dance, and soon the rain pelts down all around.

Even in these wild times, the mountain stands tall and strong, deeply rooted in the rock of Mother Earth.

For the last image, imagine the strong mountain on a winter's night. The full moon can be seen glowing between the clouds, and snowflakes drift down, each flake a unique and perfect natural wonder. Little by little, the bare trees and shrubs are sprinkled with this white powder, and some branches start to bend under their chilly burden. You can feel and smell the cold.

The mountain is a magnificent sight on this icy night. Everything about it is quiet and firm. It has long been familiar with the changing seasons and, with them, will continue to reign over us – perhaps for ever.

You, too, have experienced and survived the changing tides of emotions. If you can accept deep inside yourself that everything comes and goes, then everything becomes more bearable and you become aware of your inner strength.

4

Accept, Let Go, Change

We cannot change anything by fighting it.
Meditation helps us accept things the way they are.
Then everything changes by itself.

Affirmation

"Every day I renew my commitment to learn to let go
of self-critical thoughts. I try to avoid negative
thoughts and desires, and I live each day with more
love and patience. I look ahead to the time when
I will have left behind me much of what is
oppressing me today."

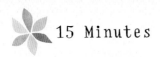

15 Minutes

Self-forgiveness meditation

By trying to forgive yourself, you are already showing
a caring attitude toward yourself. Slowly, little by little,
you can let go of your pain, your anger, your feelings of
shame and guilt. It is important that you take this vital step
toward healing and self-expression, to enable you to
genuinely like yourself again.

Go to your meditation place and sit or lie down in
a comfortable position.

Take a few deep breaths, as slowly as feels good to you.
With each inhalation, imagine you are drawing in warmth
and healing light. With every exhalation, let go of any
tension in your muscles, working slowly from the top of
your head to the soles of your feet.

Close your eyes and imagine you are in a wonderful place
of healing. Look around and then make your way, step by
step, toward a warm spring whose water you know to be
therapeutic and curative.

You can see a few people you love and cherish already sitting
in this healing water. You hear, see or simply sense that these
people are inviting you to come over.

You go over to them, sit down in the lovely warm, refreshing water and enjoy being close to these wonderful people. Some of them you know from the present, others from the past, some you may not know well. But you are connected to all of them by respect, love and trust.

Lay your head on the shoulder of one of these people, or just lean against somebody. This other person rocks you tenderly, as if you were a small child in need of protection, and it feels good.

All these dear friends and loved ones sitting in the thermal spring advise you to begin and end each day with love. This love, which you feel radiating from them, is possible because everything has been completely forgiven and you need no longer be ashamed of anything.

All these people love you just as you are. Of course we all have more to learn, and we can all benefit from letting go of certain patterns of behaviour that harm ourselves or others. All the same, you are already entirely lovable, because you are a part of this amazing universe.

And here in this warm spring pool you know that too and enjoy inner peace. When you are ready, and feeling thoroughly bathed in love and inner peace, take your leave and bring your awareness back to your body, which is fully grounded, and to your meditation place in your room. You now take this peace with you into your daily life, and you can be sure that everything that still needs doing will come more easily.

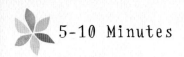 ## 5-10 Minutes

Actually, there are good things too

Rick Hanson, a neuropsychologist, always says in his lectures that negative thoughts are like Velcro, they stick fast in our brain. Good thoughts and memories, however, are like Teflon. They slip from your memory, just like that.

In this meditation we deliberately focus on the good in our life so that it can take up a larger space in our consciousness. I will give you a few thought suggestions to get you started, but of course you should also add some ideas from your own life, or replace them with your own thoughts altogether.

As ever, you start by getting yourself into a comfortable position – this time you might even lie down on your television-viewing sofa – and watch a lovely film playing inside your head.

You start by remembering any good or inspiring things you have experienced today: the rainbow over the bridge that you cross on your way to work… the old lady who gave you a friendly wave because you stopped to let her cross the road, even though she wasn't on the zebra crossing… the friendly hello from the receptionist as you arrived at the office… the delicious ice cream on the way back… Then there were the soft rays of sunshine you felt on your face as you looked up at the sky on your way home… and much more.

To begin with, you just remember this one day, and everything that was good and beautiful and touching on this particular day.

Look deep inside your heart and soul, and sense that lovely, blissful feeling you get when you are happy and thankful. What does it feel like? Where do you feel it most clearly in your body?

Now take a little more time and think back, as best you can, over the last few days. Can you manage to remember at least two or three positive experiences for each day of the last week?

You may notice that your breath has already become calmer and deeper and you have sunk into the depths of your sofa or your comfy chair. Enjoy it!

If you still have time (you may not want to stop at all), then cast your mind back over the last month or even the last year, letting it pass before you as a series of snapshots. But only pause and look at the memories that are lovely and uplifting. Try to remember the good times in as much detail as possible.

It may be, too, that you hear words from within you like "Thank you" or "Oh my God, that was great." Simply immerse yourself in your positive feelings!

I recommend writing a few notes or drawing something in your diary immediately after this exercise.

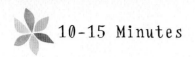

10-15 Minutes

Beneath the waterfall

Take some time for yourself and stand up straight, sit or lie down. Perhaps you have got yourself a gong or singing bowl or cymbal, and you strike it now.

Imagine yourself walking slowly through a forest or across a meadow, and eventually arriving at a waterfall.

It is a magic waterfall. You stand under it and feel the lovely water splashing down on you. This water has a purifying, strengthening effect. You feel a deep sense of gratitude that this water gives you so much joy and at the same time washes away all sadness, fear, listlessness and other negative feelings.

Now cup your hands together, collect some water and drink it. It feels refreshing and restorative.

Then cup your hands again and let the water keep raining down into them. It collects and overflows and is constantly replaced. Each drop comes and goes. Although some water always stays in your hands, you know that it is not the same water as the water that was touching you just a few seconds before. There is a constant renewal going on.

We cannot hold onto anything in life – this is the lesson you learn here under your waterfall. Everything is in constant flux. Can you begin to accept that by letting go, you allow yourself to go with the flow, and that your experience of life will keep moving on?

"Non-attachment", it is called in Buddhism. When we truly understand this, everything becomes much easier. We are then receptive, at any given moment, to new insights and experiences.

If you like you can mark the end of this contemplation by sounding a gong or cymbal again. You will feel lighter and more motivated. And you will no longer be wet, either, because your waterfall was magical.

5

Harmony with the World and All Its Beings

People who meditate are not navel-gazing and forgetting about the rest of the world. People who truly meditate are helping to bring peace, goodness and tranquillity to the world.

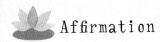 Affirmation

"May I and all beings be safe and protected, may we live in peace, and respect and support each other whenever we are able."

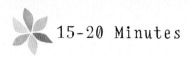 # 15-20 Minutes

Breathing for me and you

Sit down in your meditation spot and make yourself comfortable. Relax your neck and your facial muscles and gently close your eyes. Now start to breathe in and out calmly and regularly. You will start to feel how your deep breaths are supplying your whole body with oxygen and energy. Your breath touches you gently from inside and nourishes you. And when you exhale, do your best to let go of any tension.

Now let go of your breath. Let it flow naturally again, so that each breath forms a unit in itself. One inhalation and one exhalation, without taking them deeper or drawing them out longer. Simply trust your body. It is, after all, capable of carrying on breathing all by itself, even during the night, when you are asleep. Feel the growing sense of calm inside you, and the comforting warmth.

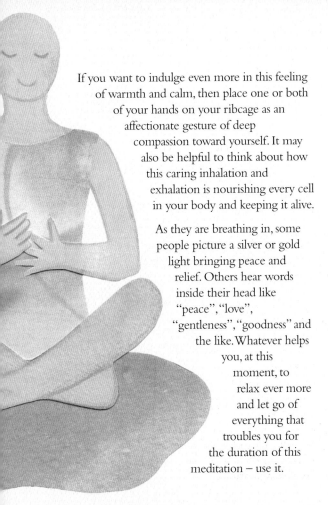

If you want to indulge even more in this feeling of warmth and calm, then place one or both of your hands on your ribcage as an affectionate gesture of deep compassion toward yourself. It may also be helpful to think about how this caring inhalation and exhalation is nourishing every cell in your body and keeping it alive.

As they are breathing in, some people picture a silver or gold light bringing peace and relief. Others hear words inside their head like "peace", "love", "gentleness", "goodness" and the like. Whatever helps you, at this moment, to relax ever more and let go of everything that troubles you for the duration of this meditation – use it.

Now I invite you to think of a person who means a lot to you, someone to whom you wish to send love, goodness and inner peace as well as to yourself. Who do you want to receive these gifts of the universe? Imagine this person now, or just see his or her name written down in your mind's eye.

Now concentrate on your exhalations. Feel how your air-filled lungs and ribcage slowly empty, and try to imagine sending this breath mixed with love and goodness to this person. You might also visualize this breath being absorbed by this dear person in the form of a silver or gold energy.

Now you are increasingly becoming one with the rhythm of your breathing, and you know that love and goodness are flowing back and forth between you and your loved one. A giving and taking is established – a wonderful exchange of uplifting energy through your breath.

This loving breath flows into you and out again like the ebb and flow of the ocean waves.

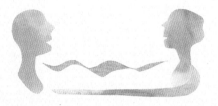

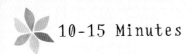

10-15 Minutes

Visit from a wise friend

I would like to tell you about Astrid. She was a very close friend of mine, whom I could talk to about anything. She introduced me to meditation when I was 19 years old, and told me about Findhorn, a lovely retreat centre in Scotland. It was all new to me, as my family did not have any interest in such things. Astrid was much older than me, the same age as my mother. But she was and remains my closest confidante as regards my spiritual salvation.

She often appears to me in this meditation. Perhaps you have someone like this in your life, who may or may not still be alive. But it could also be Gandalf, the kindly wizard from *The Lord of the Rings,* or a spiritual leader, or some other person who is an inspiration to you. It may also be an angel or spirit guide, whose presence you sense in your own way. In this meditation you can meet with him or her again.

Make your way to your meditation place or head out into nature (or imagine a peaceful place, if you happen to be out and about). Sit or lie down and make yourself comfortable, then breathe in and out deeply a few times to relax. Now close your eyes and listen.

Before long, you hear quiet footsteps and soon you can make out a figure who is familiar to you, someone you love or admire. In my case it is always Astrid. Who is it for you?

This presence has come to tell you something that has an important bearing on your life. Listen very carefully.

Afterward, this figure gives you an imaginary gift, something that means a lot to you. Accept it with gratitude. It may be of direct use, or serve as a symbolic lucky charm.

After this encounter, bid your spiritual guide a warm farewell and know that you can seek his or her help whenever you feel unsure or need advice.

How do you feel now? Relaxed, energized, content or even happy? Write down everything you have experienced in your meditation diary.

6

Life's Adventure: Creativity and Focus

It is often said that we create our own world. And it is true that everything we think, feel and do determines who we are and what course our life will take.

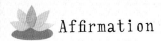 ## Affirmation

"I accept constructive criticism and address it. I reduce self-criticism to what is strictly necessary. I carry with me those insights I deem helpful. In all of this, I try my best to live in harmony with nature."

Mantra meditation

There is one particular form of meditation we have not yet looked at: the mantra. Mantras are maxims, much like affirmations, but they differ in that they do not express a certain intention, but are based on spiritual power rather than intellectual reasoning. By frequently repeating mantras, we develop inner strength and joy. Particularly when we repeat mantras in Sanskrit, Pali or Tibetan (that is to say, languages most of us don't know), we trust that texts recited billions of times through the ages will help us even when we do not understand them word for word.

Reciting mantras helps our concentration. I have a lovely mantra that I use, particularly when I am travelling or having to deal with difficult situations. I trust that it will protect me and ward off negative energies. I use this mantra in the car, on trains and planes. When I am with people, I chant it silently (to myself), but when I am alone I may chant it out loud. I always repeat the mantra three times, finishing with "Om Shanti, Shanti Shanti", which means roughly, "May the universe (or God) be sanctified."

My teacher Ursula Lyon describes mantras as a source of strength, the words consisting of "holy syllables" that can protect us. The more we cherish the mantra, the more thoroughly it protects us.

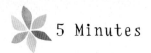 5 Minutes

Maha Mrityunjaya mantra

Sanskrit, the Indo-European language in which my favourite mantra is written, can be pronounced the way it looks. This mantra comes from the Rigveda, a yogic text, and is known as the Maha Mrityunjaya mantra. It is one of the most famous mantras handed down to us. It goes as follows:

"Om Tryambakam Yajaamahe
Sugandhim Pushtti-Vardhanam
Urvaarukamiva Bandhanaan
Mrityor Muksshiiya Maamritaat"

A literal translation is not that helpful, I find. But the meaning is roughly as follows: "We meditate on the three-dimensional reality, which penetrates and nourishes everyone like a fragrance. May we be liberated from death for the sake of immortality."

All we really need to remember is that this holy verse, which has been chanted by millions of people over thousands of years, can safeguard and protect us from danger and dark emotions.

Approach this mantra with lightness, but with trust. It is best if you are sitting or standing upright. But even if you are lying down, you should tuck your chin in slightly toward your chest and carefully stretch your spine. When you are starting out, you can simply write the syllables down several times over. As you get used to it, you can read the mantra to yourself, then out loud, and eventually, if you like, you can come up with your own tune for it.

There are myriad versions with different melodies, which of course are also available to buy or download. However, simple sequences of notes drawn from deep within you are perfectly sufficient. The more you chant the mantra, the more the sound and meaning of the words will penetrate and deeply cleanse you. Transform you, even. When we recite a mantra for a long time, our zest for life can be enhanced. We feel the vibrations throughout our body.

If you are with other people – for example, in the check-in line at the airport – silent recitation can be preferable to chanting aloud, and is just as effective. Indeed, many experts have written that mantras actually penetrate us most deeply when they are repeated purely inside our head.

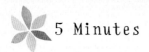 **5 Minutes**

Om mantra

If you find the whole mantra too hard to manage, you can start practising with just the syllable "Om".

It actually sounds more like AUM.

Sit down in a comfortable position, if possible on the ground, either cross-legged, in the lotus position if you are very flexible, or on a cushion with your back against a wall. The contact with the floor helps you feel grounded, rooted and strong.

Find your pitch, not too high and not too low. And then:

"Aaaaaauuummmmh"

I count about 12 to 15 beats. It will probably be fewer when you are starting out. Keep repeating this simple sound until you feel calm and firmly anchored.

It is interesting that, in all the languages I know, at least, the primal sounds uttered by babies when they are first learning to talk are the same. Most young humans start by learning to say, "ma", "mama" and so on.

Repeating any of the vowels – a, e, i, o and u – is a highly beneficial practice in general. It helps restore our balance. Try it for five minutes in your natural pitch, as quietly or loudly as you like. Again and again... You will see that it helps soothe away fear and anxiety.

Mantras miraculously connect us with the universe and all beings. They calm and nourish our soul or our higher self (or whatever you wish to call the essence of yourself, that which differentiates you from others).

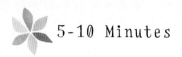

5-10 Minutes

Tree meditation

In this practice we connect with nature. There was a time
when we humans lived our lives entirely as part of nature,
and nature can still put us in touch with our true, primal
selves again, helping us to become one with the skies above
and the earth below. Over time, this can lead to us feeling a
deeper connection with Mother Earth, and more motivated
to do good to ourselves and all other living beings. And
of course it also does us good to be aware of ourselves as
part of this great universe.

Go to a park or wood and find "your" tree. For example,
I have an old oak tree near where I live. Stand in front of this
tree and gently touch its bark. Ask yourself how long it has
been there. What has it witnessed over the years? My tree
must be several hundred years old.

Now lean against the tree, either standing or seated, so that
you are touching it with one or both hands. Even when we
are right up close to the tree, its roots are directly beneath us.
Can you feel the life pulsing within the tree? Maybe, but it's
fine if you don't.

Now inhale deeply and mentally let your
breath travel all the way down into your feet,
and then deeper still right into the Earth.
Imagine the tree's roots absorbing
the energy of your
breath so that it
flows into the
whole tree.

The tree
sends this
fresh energy up
to the skies, from
where it comes
back down to you in
the form of air or
rain, entering into
you with each
new breath.

This cycle of life is constantly
repeated. Enjoy your connection to
nature and the purity of the breath,
until you feel you have drawn
enough strength from them
for today.

10 Minutes

Dance of life

I was inspired to practise dance meditation at a one-week course with Petra Klein on Tenerife about 15 years ago. Through it I learned how to get to know myself better and bring my body, mind and soul into harmony.

Anyone can dance – I'm talking about free dance here, the kind you often see young children doing. What we experience in these moments is then somehow carried through into our "serious" life: light-heartedness, devotion, happiness, a sense of flow. Sigmund Freud himself said that we need to regress every day (in other words, behave like a child) to keep our mind in balance. This form of meditation can also help us bring subconscious needs or psychological damage to the surface and thereby heal ourselves. So:

Choose a soothing, tranquil piece of music. Stand in the middle of the room (alone and undisturbed) and start swaying from left to right in time with the gentle rhythms, like leaves in a soft breeze. Use your whole body: trunk, legs, arms, shoulders, back, hips, pelvis, chest, neck, head. Just let

yourself be propelled by the music, and feel that
you exist, that you matter and are important, a
part of this wonderful creation.

Now choose a more energetic piece of music,
something with drums, cymbals, xylophones or other
percussion instruments. I like to use Balinese, African
or South American music. You can let yourself go even
more this time. You can make wilder movements,
maybe jump in the air, shake your body, speed up your
dancing, incorporate double-quick steps, clap your hands or
sing along. You can and must express yourself completely
freely, from the depths of your soul. Keep dancing until you
feel liberated and refreshed.

Afterward, you are welcome to put on some really soothing
music – perhaps Santana on electric guitar, or relaxing
violins – to create a kind of calm after the storm. You can
embrace yourself with a tender squeeze or just sit or lie
down and let yourself be embraced by the music and
the rhythms.

This meditation allows us to let go of our shyness, our
inhibitions. We feel the child in ourselves, who expresses
him- or herself completely naturally and freely, no matter
what others may think. This meditation can help you gain in
self-acceptance and self-assurance. We find energy and
creativity in ourselves.

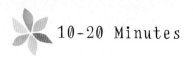

10-20 Minutes

Inspiration meditation

This meditation exercise is especially useful for picturing and creating a worthwhile future for yourself. Take yourself off to a quiet, peaceful room where you can listen to music. I would suggest not using headphones – let the music flow freely around the whole room instead. You don't need a perfect sound system for this, it's just a matter of having some peaceful, quiet music in the background. Mozart, Bach, the rhythms of nature, anything that can put you in an inwardly calm but also alert state of mind.

This time you might also like to get yourself a nice mug of herbal tea and maybe some chocolate, anything that will put you in a cheerful mood. The room should have a large table, or just an area of floor space that is free of furniture, where you have room to lay out a large piece of paper. You should also get out some coloured pens. If you have a much-loved pet that is able to sit still for a while and just be stroked, then invite it into this creative space with you.

Now you are ready to embark on your playful journey of discovery. To start with, just listen to the music, and sit down and make yourself comfortable, with the paper in front of you. The pens are next to the paper, and you close your eyes and breathe in and breathe out… in and out…

And now ask yourself the following questions: "What do I really want to do next in my life? What do I really want, what do I actually need, what do I dearly wish for?"

Listen to the music and pick up a pen, any colour you like. Whenever a word or phrase occurs to you, write it down. (You can open your eyes for this, of course.) Whether the ideas that pop up make sense or not, whether there is any connection between them or not – simply write them down. Change the colour of your pen once in a while. Breathe, listen, delve into yourself without having any particular expectations. Immerse yourself in the river of creative energy and dive for your treasure – whether it's a matter of finding a new job, meeting interesting people or taking up a new hobby.

Stay in this energized state for 10 to 20 minutes. When you feel it is enough for today, bring this creative meditation to a close. Please don't read everything immediately or try to piece it together into a story or decision.

Repeat this exercise three to seven times over the course of a week. Once you have covered several sheets of paper with writing, read through the ideas that have surfaced from your subconscious. Sometimes in silence, and sometimes with your background music playing. It is very likely that you will now be able to make sense of these words and phrases, that you will see in them a signpost, a new goal. Not everything has to feel logical or final at this stage, but a pointer will at least be visible.

Concluding Words

We have now reached the end of this little book. I have introduced you to a whole series of meditations, affirmations, visualizations, movement sequences and mantras.

I very much hope that, once you have had an initial browse through, you find something you would like to try out. Give yourself an affectionate little nudge and just try it. You might even start with the exercise that strikes you as particularly unusual or strange. You never know what might lie beyond this first impression.

To finish, I am going to teach you a meditation I learned from my teacher Ursula Lyon. She warmly recommended it to me, because there is great potential in its simplicity.

This meditation has the power to help you attain inner calm and peace of mind.

Ursula says that you only have a real sense of your own being if you are in touch with your body. And this meditation, originally from Myanmar, helps put you in touch with it.

In our mind's eye, we repeatedly touch eight parts of our body… a simple number, not too high, which nevertheless prevents the mind from thinking about problems and to-do lists. The repetitive nature of the sequence helps settle a hyperactive mind and eventually brings it to a state of calm. This is a meditation that can be done anytime, anywhere.

Eight-point meditation

Sit down in your place of meditation. Choose a position that you can comfortably stay in for 15 to 30 minutes.

Begin by saying to yourself, in your head: "Here I sit, safe and upright, with humility."

Start with your right foot and silently repeat these words: "Here is my right foot. I feel it or know that it is there."

Then turn your attention to your right knee: once again, notice, feel or know that it is there.

Then move your attention up to the right buttock. Again, notice, feel, know that it is there.

Now take your awareness to your left foot: notice, feel, know that it is there.

Next to the left knee: notice, feel, know that it is there.

Now to the left buttock: notice, feel, know that it is there.

Now move on to the right hand: you notice, feel and know that it is resting in your lap.

Then comes the left hand: notice, feel, know that it is there.

These are the eight points. Finally, bring your attention to your tailbone. Breathe in very calmly and as you do so, take your attention all the way up your spine to your neck. Have a long, deep exhale and take your attention back down from your neck to your tailbone.

You can repeat the entire sequence as many times as you like.

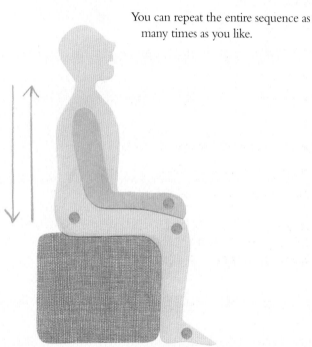

The eight-point meditation in brief

- right foot
- right knee
- right buttock
- left foot
- left knee
- left buttock
- right hand
- left hand
- inhale: from tailbone to neck
- exhale: from neck to tailbone

After your practice you will feel more focused and energized, but in a calm, relaxed way. This is an ideal starting exercise for when you want to be creative and not let your thoughts wander. It will also enable you to gain a clearer idea of what you want to work on mentally or emotionally.

Meditation creates harmony

By alternately focusing and letting go, we are able to gradually resolve both internal and external conflicts and slowly restore our balance. Meditation helps us to perceive life's little wonders – to see them, feel them or even hear them. On this journey, embrace true life, for only then will you really feel part of it, appreciate and value it, and be keen to protect it.

May you feel safe and loved.
May you experience and accept the joy and adventure
of your existence with deep humility and gratitude.

Acknowledgements

I want to thank Ursula Lyon for teaching me Meditation and Compassion, and for passing on her deep wisdom. I also want to thank my dear husband Bernhard for supporting me in many ways during the process of writing.

Last but not least my thanks go to all the people involved in making this book: the illustrator Jenny Römisch and all the editors, designers and production managers, whose support is so very important for being creative and making this wonderful book possible.